D1443842

Games with
Sticks, Stones and Shells

THE MARSHALL CAVENDISH ILLUSTRATED GUIDE TO

GAMES CHILDREN PLAY AROUND THE WORLD

Games with Sticks, Stones and Shells

Ruth Oakley
Illustrated by Steve Lucas

Marshall Cavendish
New York · London · Toronto · Sydney

Library Edition 1989

© Marshall Cavendish Limited 1989
© DPM Services Limited 1989

Published by Marshall Cavendish Corporation
            147 West Merrick Road
            Freeport
            Long Island
            N.Y. 11520

Produced by DPM Services Limited
Designed by Graham Beehag

Library of Congress Cataloging-in-Publication Data

Oakley, Ruth,
    Games with Sticks and Stones/written by Ruth Oakley:
Illustrated by Steve Lucas.
        p.   cm. −(Games children play)
        Includes index.
        Summary: Gives the background and instructions for playing
hopscotch, jacks, and a variety of games played with sticks, stones
and marbles.
        ISBN 1-85435-079-X:
        1. Games-Juvenile literature. 2. Marbles (Game)−Juvenile
literature. 3. Hopscotch−Juvenile literature. 4. Staffs (Sticks,
canes, etc.)−Juvenile literature. 5. Jacks (Game)−Juvenile
literature. [1. Games.] I, Lucas, Steve, [1]. II. Title.
III. Series: Oakley, Ruth. Games children play.
GV1203.027 1989   88-28773
796.2-dc19   CIP
                                                             AC

ISBN 1-85435-076-5 (set)

Printed and bound in Italy by L.E.G.O. SpA, Vicenza

Contents

Sticks and Stones

One of the reasons for man's progress was his ability to use natural objects as tools. Although there are some apes and monkeys that use sticks and stones as weapons or tools, such behavior is not common in the animal kingdom. Play is fun, but it is also the way in which young animals, including humans, learn.

Throwing sticks is a game which children play all over the world, just as they probably have always done. The Tuaregs, nomadic Arabs from North Africa, have contests to see who can throw a pointed stick or javelin the highest or farthest. To judge the height, they hop while throwing and the number of hops between the throwing of the stick and its landing determines who wins.

The Sioux Indians in North America had similar contests in the snow. They used sticks with feathers on the end as flights to improve the accuracy. The aim was to see who could throw the stick the farthest by letting it slide along the ground as it landed.

Children along the Mississippi throw long, pointed sticks in the raised-earth banks, or levees, of the river. It can be played as an individual challenge of skill or as a team game.

Herqr Relay Race is a team game which has its origins in the Nordic custom of shooting an arrow (*herqr*) to announce the coming of an enemy and to warn one's allies to prepare for war.

You need a fairly large space, indoors or outside, to play this game. Mark a goal line; then draw two large circles which just touch this line and are about a yard apart. In the circles,

The layout for Herqr Relay Race.

6

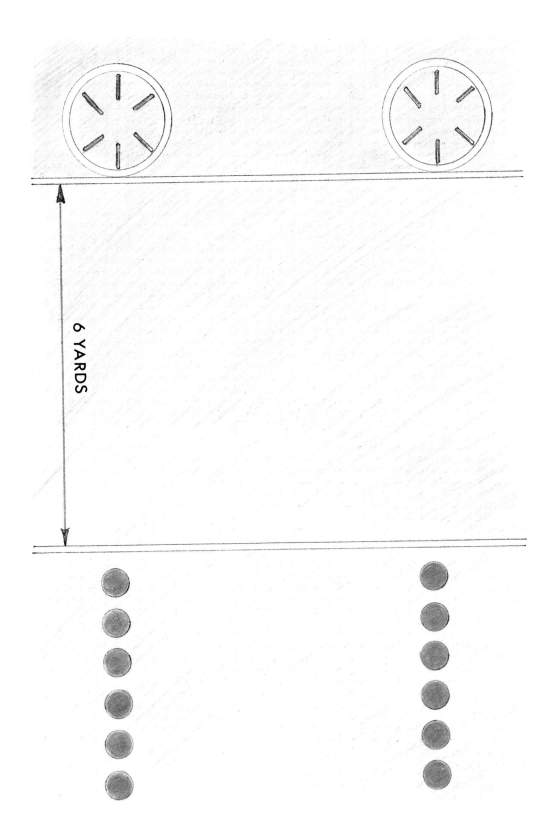

6 YARDS

place one stick for each player on each team. Mark another line parallel to the goal line about 6 yards away from it. Two equal teams of players line up, one behind the other, with the leader of each team just behind the starting line.

A time limit is agreed, and the timekeeper gives the signal to begin. On the signal, the first player from each team runs to his team's circle, picks up a stick, and runs back with it to the next person in the team. The second player runs to the circles with the stick, drops it into the other team's circle, picks up

another stick out of his own circle, and runs back to the starting line to hand it to the next player. The game continues until the timekeeper calls time; the team with the fewest arrows in its circle is the winning one.

Greek children play a game on the beach called **Hook the Driftwood Stick.** A stick is placed at an agreed distance away from a line in soft dry sand, and they try to drag it towards them using an old cup with a piece of string tied to it.

A similar party game is **Indoor Fishing.** Make some fishing rods; tie pieces of string to garden canes or pieces of doweling and tie a paper clip which has been opened out to make a hook on the end of each one. Place an old sheet or similar piece of material on the floor to represent the sea. Cut out a variety of fish from cardboard; insert a safety pin through the nose of each one so it can be "hooked." Make them different shapes and sizes; assign them different score values; and place them in the "sea." The game can either be played individually or as teams.

Witti Dandu is a game from India which is played during celebrations following religious ceremonies to celebrate the birthday of the god Krishna. The "dandu" is a piece of wood about an inch in diameter and about 2 feet long with a notch at one end. The "witti" is another piece of wood about 8 inches long with points at each end. To play, dig a trench in the ground for the Dandu to lie in at an angle with its notch at

ground level, and place the witti across the hole. One player then stamps on the dandu to make the witti fly up into the air. The other player tries to catch the witti and throw it back into the hole while the first player tries to hit the witti with the dandu and stop it from landing in the hole.

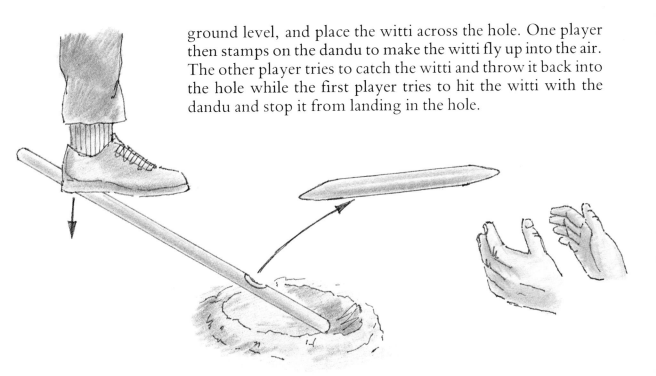

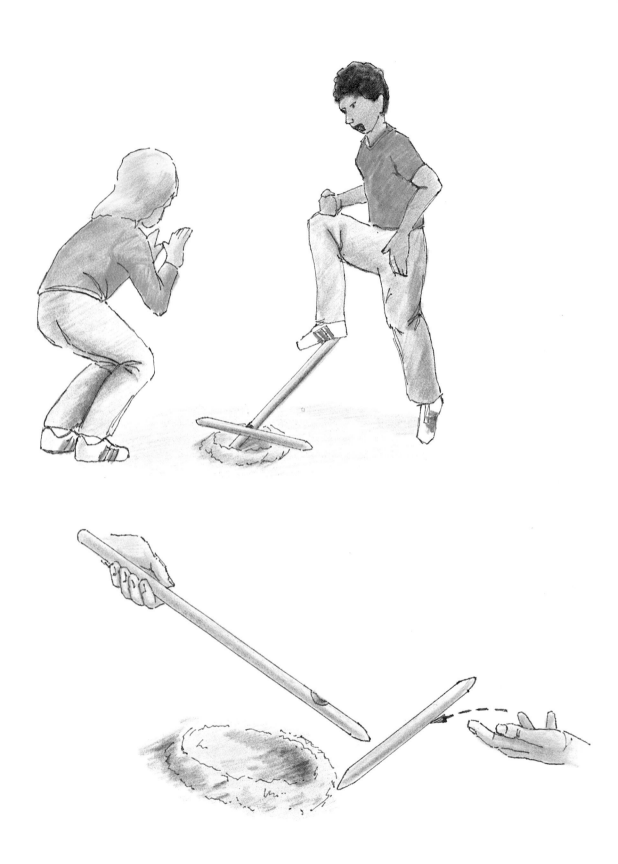

If the witti lands within 6 inches of the hole, the first player is out, the second player becomes the stamper, and a third player tries to catch the witti. The players agree beforehand on a system of scoring points for catching the witti and getting it in the hole.

Tahteab is an ancient Egyptian game which is usually played by young men during festivals, or at clubs or in school. Each of the two players needs a strong bamboo cane about two

yards long which has had the ends rounded off. The idea of the game is to touch the other player with the stick. Only touches above the waist count: touches below the waist, and hitting or stricking hard, are fouls. The stick must be held with both hands between touches.

The system of scoring is agreed before the start, and a judge referees and keeps score. It can be played as an individual or as a team game. To play as a team, each pair competes, and the scores are totaled for the team.

Another game from Egypt which is played with sticks is played in a circle. Each player has a stick about one and a half yards long and stands about three yards away from her neighbors, facing the middle of the circle and holding her stick upright with one end on the floor. At a given signal, each player leaves her stick and races to the next one on her right to try to catch it before it falls. If she fails, she is out, and her stick is removed from the circle. The winner is the last person remaining at the end of the game.

A game with sticks and stones which comes from Iran is called **Nomads and Settlers.** The players divide into two equal teams. The Settlers gather as many sticks and stones as

they can find and place them in a large circle drawn on the ground. Then they join hands around the circle to try to stop the Nomads from entering it. The Nomads draw another circle around the Settlers' circle, about three yards from the inner circle. This space between the two circles is No Man's Land.

The Nomads charge from their territory and try to dodge between the Settlers to steal their sticks and stones. The Nomads are not allowed to use their hands to get past the Settlers; they can only push with their heads and shoulders.

If a Nomad gets in the circle, he must be allowed out with his booty, but once he is out of No Man's Land, he can be chased and captured by being touched with the palms of both hands.

The game ends either when all the Nomads have been captured or all the sticks and stones have been taken.

Children make up games using whatever is around them, and in most places, stones can be found. One of the simplest games is to set up an empty can or a pile of stones and take turns in trying to hit it with a stone from an agreed distance. Another popular idea is to draw a circle on the ground, put a stone inside the circle, and try to knock it out with another one.

In China, children play a team game with sticks called **Lame Chicken.** For each team, ten sticks are laid on the ground about a foot apart, parallel to each other like the rungs of a ladder. The teams line up behind each other, about five yards away from the first stick. At a signal, the first player from each team hops up to the sticks, hops over them one at a time, picks up the last one, hops back with it and places it at the beginning. Then, the next player does the same, and so

on, until every member of the team has hopped through the ladder. The winning team is the one that completes the sequence first.

Children in China play **Chuck Stone.** This is a game for any age and for any number of players. Three or more piles of small stones are placed in a row about a foot apart. Each player has to say which pile and stone he is aiming at before he throws his stone. If he hits his target, he keeps it and has another turn until he misses. As the piles get knocked down, the odd stones remain where they are and become targets. The winner is the one with the most stones at the end.

In Belgium, children play **Baton Maudit,** a game which is similar to Pass the Parcel and Consequences. A stick is passed around a circle of children sitting on the ground. One child is blindfolded in the middle of the circle; when she whistles, whoever is holding the baton or stick at the time has to do a consequence.

Boys in Pakistan and India play **Gulli Danda.** The "gulli" is a piece of stick which is cylindrical in the middle and tapered at the ends. It is about 2 inches wide and 4 inches long. The "danda" is another stick about 2 feet long. Children often make their own equipment from the trees for this game.

Gulli Danda is usually played outside and can be played individually or in teams. A circle about a yard in diameter is drawn on the ground, and the gulli is placed in its center. The players stand about three yards away from the circumference of the circle. The members of the batting team take it in turn to go into the circle and hit the gulli hard with the danda so that the gulli flies up into the air. While it is in the air, the gulli is hit with the danda as far as possible.

If the gulli is caught by a member of the fielding team, the batter is out. If the gulli is not caught, the batter lays the danda in the circle and the fielder, standing where the gulli fell, throws it at the danda. If the danda is hit, the batter is out. If the fielder misses, the batter has another turn until he is caught or thrown out. Scoring is done either according to how many hits are made or to how far the gulli is hit.

Nekki is a traditional children's game from Japan. A tree branch or bamboo cane about a foot long with a point at one end is stuck in the ground. The players stand behind a throwing line and take turns to try to knock over the upright stick by throwing their own sticks at it. This is an old game which may have originally been played when the "nekki," the piece of wood which supported the traditional New Year's pine and bamboo decoration, was driven into the ground.

O Krotalias is a game Greek children play with a tin box with a pebble inside it. You could use an empty drink can instead of the box. One of you holds the box and is called the krotalis, or "rattlesnake." The rest of the players are blindfolded, and when they hear the sound of the pebble being shaken in the box, they have to run forward and touch the "rattlesnake." When a player manages to do so, she becomes the new "rattlesnake."

If you are lucky enough to have a beach or lakeshore to play on, no doubt you have had fun seeing how far out you can

Flat, smooth pebbles are best for spinning.

throw a stone. If you practice spinning your stone, you can make it hop across the water before it sinks. You can compete with your friends to see who can get the most hops, or you can set yourself a challenge to beat your own record.

Shells on the beach are also fascinating and are used in games by children in many countries. In Malaysia and Indonesia, girls play **Kulit K'rang.** They sit in a circle with a bowl in the middle, and each player has twenty cockleshells. They take turns to put a shell on the back of their hands, toss it up into the air, pick up another one, and catch the tossed shell as it comes down. If they drop either of the shells, they have to put a shell in the bowl in the middle. The last player to have a shell left is the winner.

Marbles

No doubt the first marbles were smooth, round pebbles, and some which have been found in neolithic ruins and burial sites are thought to have been used in games. Ancient Egyptian marbles can be seen in museums in various parts of the world. The Romans had many pastimes involving nuts, which had similar rules to games played with marbles. In some parts of the world, the stones from fruit like peaches and apricots are still used.

In China, **Ishihajiki** was a game played at court by the nobility. Small pebbles were flicked to hit each other. The game was introduced into Japan, where it is still played today under the name of **Ohajiki,** although flat pieces of glass or plastic are used instead of stones.

A glass stoppered bottle. The marble can be clearly seen in the neck.

High bounce balls can also be used for playing marbles.

In Victorian times, marble games were very popular in England and the United States, and they are still played today in countries as far apart as Africa and Ireland. The sight of children playing marbles is regarded as a sure sign of spring.

There is something very satisfying about the feel of a smooth, round glass marble, and about the fact that each one has its own unique pattern and coloring. Agate marbles, or "aggies" are collectors' items today. Before bottles had metal tops, they had glass stoppers. Children used them as marbles and called them "glassys," which was short for "glasseyes." The most common marbles today are made of glass with colored swirls inside them. They come in different sizes. Ball bearings are also popular and are called "steelies." You can make your own marbles, called "marrididdles," by rolling and baking clay.

There are very many games to play with marbles, and no doubt you can make up your own. One of the most common, which is played throughout the world from Thailand and Burma to Europe and which is probably one of the oldest, is called **Ring Taw** in Britain. A ring about half a yard in diameter is drawn on the ground. A "taw line" is drawn two or three yards away from the circle. Each player puts an agreed number of marbles in the ring and then in turn each flicks one of her marbles at the marbles in the ring and tries to

knock as many of the marbles out of the ring as she can. She is allowed to keep the marbles which she has knocked out of the ring, but if her own marble remains inside the ring, it is "fat" and has to stay in the ring. She can, however, carry on flicking with the marbles she has just won until she fails to hit any marbles. Then it is the next player's turn. After the player's first turn, if her marble stays inside the ring, she has to leave it there, and she has to replace the marbles she knocked out on that turn.

To flick a marble, bend your index finger to make a cradle for the marble and then flick it with your thumb. You have to "knuckle down," which means that you must keep the middle joint of your index finger on the ground.

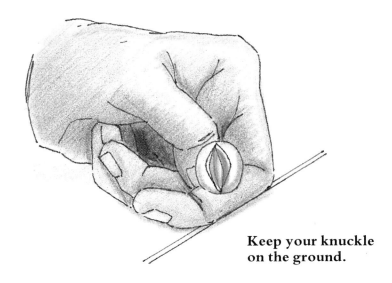

Keep your knuckle on the ground.

Bombers, Tearing Up the Pea Patch, Nucis (Nuts), and **Bounce-eye** are different names for the same game. Make a circle as for Ring Taw, but the players stand around the edge of it and drop their marbles in turn from eye height and try to "bomb" the marbles which have been placed in the center. The marbles which a player knocks out of the ring become his. **Stand Up Megs** is similar, but players stand about two yards away on a line and throw marbles at a target in the ring.

Another ring game with marbles is **Pyramid.** One player makes a pile with his marbles in the ring. Fourteen is a good number, because you can have three rows of three with a square of four on top of that and then one marble on the top. The owner of the pyramid then charges each of the other players one marble to have a shot at it. If the shooter hits any of the pyramid marbles out of the ring, they become hers.

To play **Hit and Span, Bossout,** or **Going to School,** one player rolls his marble any distance he wishes and the next player aims his marble at the first one, which is then called the "jack." If he hits the jack or rolls his marble near enough to "span" it, he can claim it. To span it means to be able to touch

Playing Bombers

Playing Pyramids

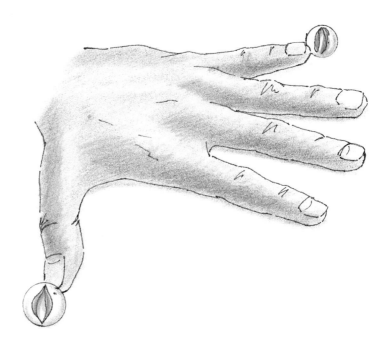

one marble with the thumb and the other with the little finger. If he misses, both marbles stay and the second player's marble becomes the new jack. When a player succeeds in hitting or spanning the jack, he claims all the marbles that are in play at the time.

In **Spangie,** one player flicks her marble against a wall, the next player does the same and tries to span the first marble. Either she succeeds and takes both marbles, or they continue until a player can span the last marble that has been flicked. She then takes all the marbles that are in play.

Playing *Spangie*.

In the Italian version of this game, players stand with their backs to the wall and throw the marbles between their legs at the wall, aiming to get as close as possible to a line drawn about a yard away from the wall.

Marbles are placed along a line with about 2 inches between each one to play **Stroke, Plum Pudding,** or **Picking Plums.** Players stand on a line at an agreed distance away from the marbles, and they aim at them by flicking. If someone knocks a marble off the line, he keeps it.

There are also marbles games in which holes are made in the ground and the players try to sink their marbles in the holes.

Similarly, you can make a marble arch with different scores on the openings. In the north of England, children use the indentations on manhole covers as targets with different scores.

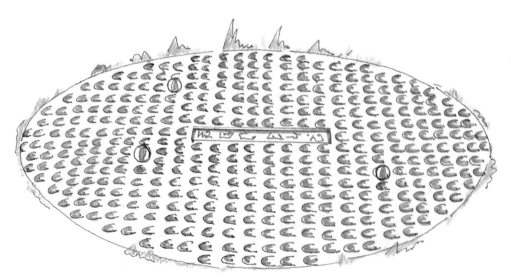

Solitaire is a traditional marble game played in Great Britain, which is similar to the U.S. game called Hig. It has a board with thirty-three depressions, holding thirty-two marbles. The middle hole is left empty. The object of the game is to end up with only one marble, preferably in the center hole. Marbles are removed by jumping over one another into an empty space.

A typical Solitaire board.

Hopscotch

As with so many of the games which children play the world over, hopscotch is an extremely ancient game. It is believed to have originated in Asia and the playing patterns, or "beds," may have represented the journey through life from birth to death, or the journey from Hell to Heaven or Paradise. There are hopscotch patterns scratched on the pavements of the Forum in Rome. The game appears in many guises and has different names in various countries, but the basic idea of hopping in a special order around a pattern drawn on the ground and without touching any of the lines is common to them all.

Hopscotch is the English name for the game. "Scotch" has nothing to do with Scotland, but comes from the verb "to scotch," which means "to scratch" or "score" a pattern onto a surface. In Ireland, it is called Beds, or Scotch Hop. In Germany, it is Hinkspiel, the hopping game. The Dutch call it Hinkelbaan, and the Danish Hopskok. Rayuela is the Argentinian name, and in Vietnam, where it is played in pairs, it is known as Pico. The French call it Marelles, and in India, it is Ekaria Dukaria. The game is also known in Russia, Scandinavia, and China. In China, it is played simply as a series of jumps without a marker being thrown.

In most other countries, a stone or similar object, which also has local names, is thrown into the bed as part of the game. It can be called a "potsie," a "chaney," a "piggy," a "piccy," or a "scottie.'

There are many different traditional patterns for the bed, some of which are shown, but there is no reason why you can not make up your own for your locality.

The rules of play are also varied, and you can adapt them to suit yourself. This is one way of playing using the simplest diagram of just five rectangles numbered one to five. First, walk through the five rectangles and back again with a flat stone balanced on the back of your hand and without touching a line. Then throw the stone into the first rectangle (it must not touch a line). Hop through the rectangles and back, putting only one foot on the ground all the way through and without touching any lines. Pick up your stone when you return to the first rectangle.

Throw the stone into the second rectangle and repeat the

1

2

procedure. Then throw the stone into the third rectangle and so on until you throw your stone into the fifth rectangle. When you have hopped to rectangle five, pick up your stone and throw it into rectangle one. Hop through to one, pick up the stone, balance the stone on the back of your thumb, and hop back to five.

Throw into space two from space five. Hop through to two, pick up the stone, balance it on one eyelid with your head tilted back, and hop back to five. Throw into space three

3

4

and hop to one with it in the palm of your hand. Throw the stone from one into four, hop to four, and return to one with the stone on your head. Finally, thrown the stone into space five, hop through, and return with the stone balanced on your back.

If you step on a line, drop the stone, or get the order wrong at any stage, you are out, and the next player has a turn. Also, each time you get home with the stone, you have to drop it into the palm of your hand, throw it up, and catch it.

Another common variation is to kick the stone from one space to the next with your hopping foot as you hop through the bed. If you play this way, score points for how far you get through the bed before you or the stone touches a line.

With the jumping pattern, throw the stone into one, hop into one and pick up the stone and then jump into three and four with one foot in each simultaneously. Repeat this for four, five, and six. Then repeat the sequence from the beginning, but, instead of just carrying the stone when you have picked it up out of space one, carry it in the ways previously described in an order agreed among the players.

Jackstones is a variation of jacks for which no ball is needed. The basic equipment is five stones or five jacks. Nowadays, jacks are made out of metal or plastic, but their knobbly shape is derived from the fact that the game was originally played with the knucklebones from the knee joint of a sheep. In coastal areas, it was sometimes played with whelk shells. In Staffordshire, an iron and steel making area of England, boys used pieces of round iron punched out of boiler plates.

Roman knucklebones beautifully decorated with inlaid amber and precious stones have been found. The Romans also had sets made of bronze, glass, and alabaster.

The Romans seem to have encouraged the spread of this pastime across the world. It probably originated in Japan where it was known as Tedama. In ancient Greece, it was called Pentalitha. There is a statue in the British Museum of two Roman boys playing Tali, or Chios. The Romans introduced the game to Europe, and it is played in Great Britain and Ireland.

The song "This old man" may have been part of the Irish way of playing the game. It goes:

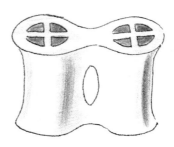

> *This old man*
> *He played one.*
> *He played nick nack on my drum.*
> *Nick nack Paddy whack*
> *Give a dog a bone*
> *This old man came rolling home.*
> CHORUS
> *Nick nack Paddy whack*
> *Give a dog a bone*
> *This old man came rolling home.*
> In the succeeding verses you say:
> *This old man*
> *He played two*
> *He played nick nack on my shoe.*

and so on.

On the Scottish island of Arran, the game is called Sgreaga.

From Europe, it later traveled to North and South America. In South America and Haiti, it is known as Cantillos. Children in the U.S. call it Otadama, or Japanese Jacks. The Arab version called Kaab is played in Saudi Arabia, and the Chinese call it Chance Bone.

Fivestones can be played indoors or out. You just need a level ground surface. Up to about four people play; if there are too many people, each player has to wait a long time for a turn. Each person has a turn to try to repeat a sequence of moves without making a mistake or dropping a stone at the wrong time. There are traditional ways of playing, but as with all these games, there is no reason why you should not make up your own.

To play **Dabs,** squat down on your haunches and put five jacks or stones on the back of your hand. Throw them up and catch them on the back of your hand.

Then flick your hand from the wrist to throw the jacks up from the back of your hand and catch them in your palm.

For the next round, leave four of the jacks on the ground, throw up the one remaining jack, and pick up one of the jacks

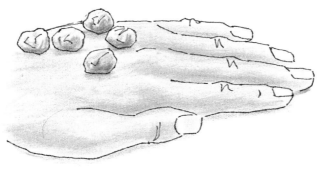

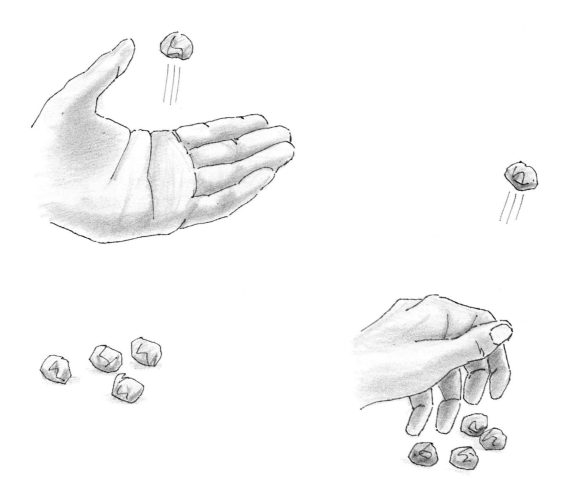

on the ground before you catch the thrown jack again. While still holding in your hand the jack you have just picked up, repeat the action until, one at a time, you have picked up the other three jacks which are still on the ground.

Put four of the jacks back on the ground. Throw up or "sky" the one in your hand and, before you catch it as it falls, pick up two of the jacks on the ground. Hold the two jacks in your hand and repeat the move and you will have all five in your hand again.

For the next round, called Horse and Cart, first pick up one jack, the Horse, and then three more for the Cart.

Next, take all four of the stones from the ground in one snatch while "skying" the fifth.

If you like, you can then repeat the first sequence with all five jacks and go through all the moves again, but this time keep all the jacks in your hand each time and throw them down one at a time, two at a time, and so on, instead of picking them up.

If at any time you make a mistake in the sequence or drop a jack, you are out and the next person has a turn.

Another way of playing is to mark stones with letters and to make words by picking them up one at a time in the correct order while you throw up a jack.

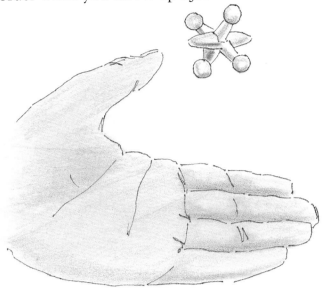

Glossary

agate   A semi-precious stone; a kind of quartz.

allies   Friends; people who are on the same side in a war.

booty   Goods and possessions, usually taken by force.

circumference   The distance around the edge of a circle.

cylindrical   Shaped like a cylinder; i.e., having straight sides and a circular cross section. A tin can is usually cylindrical in shape.

diameter   Any line which passes through the center of the circle and joins together two points on the circumference of the circle.

Forum, The   The central meeting place in Ancient Rome.

Krishna   A Hindu god.

neolithic   Belonging to the Stone Age.

nomads, nomadic   People who do not build villages and towns to live in and who do not settle in one place. They move around a country and usually live by hunting. They often live in tents because these homes can easily be put up, taken down, and carried from place to place.

Nordic   Coming from Scandinavia.

parallel   Two lines are parallel if the distance between them always remains the same. Parallel lines will never meet.

tapered   Gradually becoming thinner.

Index of Countries

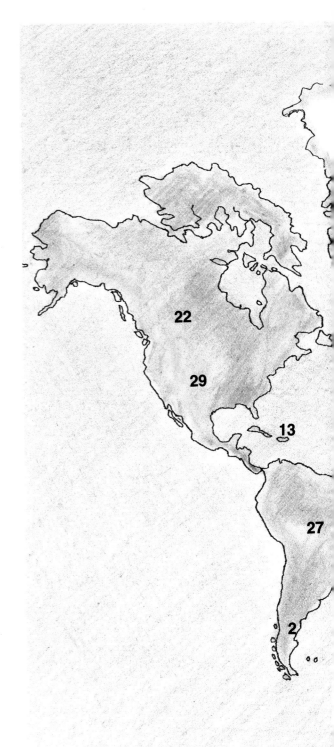

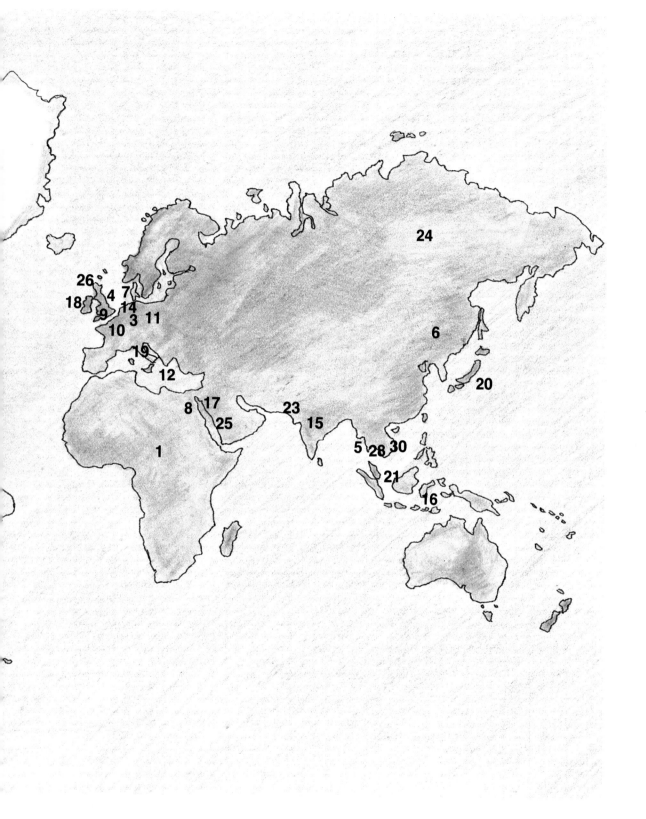

Index